"POP" Pops the Popcorn

Written by Bob Egan • Illustrated by Paige Billin-Frye

Bob puts some popcorn in the pot.
He puts in a little.

2

He puts in a lot.

"POP" pops the popcorn.

4

Stop, Bob, stop!
The popcorn is popping over the top.

Get a box.
Get a mop.
The popcorn is popping over the top.

"POP" pops the popcorn.
When will it stop?

We don't care.
We like it a lot.